Michael Farrell | Family Trees

Poetry books by Michael Farrell

ode ode

BREAK ME OUCH

a raiders guide

open sesame

Cocky's Joy

A Lyrebird: Selected Poems (US)

I Love Poetry

GIRAMONDO POETS

Michael Farrell | Family Trees

First published 2020
from the Writing and Society Research Centre
at Western Sydney University
by the Giramondo Publishing Company
PO Box 752
Artarmon NSW 1570 Australia
www.giramondopublishing.com

Designed by Harry Williamson
Typeset by Andrew Davies
in 10/16.5 pt Baskerville BT
Cover design by Jenny Grigg

Printed and bound by Ligare Book Printers
Distributed in Australia by NewSouth Books

A catalogue record for this
book is available from the
National Library of Australia.

ISBN: 978-1-925818-40-6

9 8 7 6 5 4 3 2 1

Contents

Good Fortune

Suddenly I was a banker with a magnificent desk
Yet it seemed that after years of success and luck
Everything I'd worked for was about to disappear
Due to mismanagement or fraud or the economy
Thanks to good fortune however it turned around
And I kept the desk with its four kangaroo legs

Suddenly I was a farmer with a magnificent flock
Yet it seemed that the good seasons and high yields
Everything I'd taken for granted had now collapsed
Due to climate change or new bureaucratic guidelines
Thanks to good fortune though I was able to sell it
And it became a sanctuary for sheep with wooden legs

Suddenly I was a toymaker with a magnificent factory
Yet it seemed after years of innovation and record sales
Everything had become unpopular and old-fashioned
Due to multinational pressure or the cheapness of plastic
Thanks to good fortune or rep I got a new commission
And became a maker of robots with weaponised legs

Suddenly I was a priest with a magnificent window
Yet it seemed that the amount of joy and worshippers
Everything that seemed right in the world, was dwindling
Due to scandals and competing with Twitter and Satan
Thanks to good fortune or God's grace or Coca-Cola
And the thirst for promotion, I became a Coke on legs

Suddenly I was a porn star with a magnificent action
Yet it seemed that the decades of sex and recognition
Everything that'd once been a stud's due, was over
Due to ageing or cams and the rise of amateurism
Thanks to good fortune or surgery I literally became
A donkey and could do so much more with four legs

Suddenly I was a kangaroo with a magnificent head
Yet it seemed that after years of a cushioned existence
Everything in the building including me was obsolete
Due to mismanagement or asbestos or the economy
Thanks to good fortune I was reprieved (and relieved)
And went to the home of a creature with two legs

Suddenly no one believed in magnificence any more
Yet everything that once had legs was due to return
Thanks to good fortune and the decline of the wheel

G'dayology

Or this: I have an autistic child, and
when she repeats the whole Catholic
Mass at lunch the medical team call it
echolalia. Dock their lunch says Bruce
say hello to reverse red tape prejudice

The trees won't chop themselves down
unless you show them patiently, by
analogy. We had to gaol your combine
harvester the police say, it was doing
something wrong. It was Sunday but

I have a prosthetic arm so I chisel my way
in to the yard. Write a speech for Stump
Week: it's not complimentary to your
Christmas lights or the way you arrange
white bread in a summer pudding

Someone's visor slips out of the op-shop
Ghosts don't vote or they'd scare the
Liberal Party. My voice caught in a
wombat burrow by the time the night's
over. Coral's gutless that's its problem

Practically by definition, a predator's
unseen till too late. Bruce is an asset. No

matter how much nothing there is to do
he's always done the least. He was in no
rush for a handbag made from a native

bird. The young bull in love with his
father in the mirror and his mother in his
sister. Classic husbandry. In the paranoid
waiting room, the weather's a major
distraction, the TV appears to think

Speech patterns flatten this route, raise
another. The gate indicates all kinds of
inclusions, performing none. Religious
fallback itself begins to fall. I have an
autistic lyrebird that covers its head when

we go to bed. The kids are braver than
if raised on abstract mammals. Up a ridge
and down a gullet. No, I won a bag of
coal but won't burn it, that'll show the
desert. I wanted to show my upset sister

how family war's an antidote to the world
She took the glockenspiel from my hand
and sang a g'day that cracked the water
tower, raked the hay, shaded the arvo sun
and set the snake and mongoose free

Folktales Of The Avant-Garde

Who will we talk about?   The horse with the golden mane?
That possessed a back so flat it was used as an ironing board
That was made out of poppies and trotted on roads like a fish
And was though a gelding as smart and as fast as a wombat
Every movement needs a leader every leader needs a chair
Every camp needs a fire and every campfire entertainment
At the time it seemed like a break later it seems like a hiccup
We toss the remains of dinner into the flames when finished
The horse tells us a story about an outlaw sworn to celibacy
We Irish try to make sense of by cutting up the newspaper
Owls appear on branches or the ground never at eye level
Reckless coves stick swans to their heads as they enter lake

Who will we talk about?   The roo with a fake moustache?
Fools yearn for an alchemist to turn old ploughs into gold
They walked out of the pear grove whistling an Italian tune
Wearing a barbecue apron so their sexes remained private
Any dog that came within range was turned into a rosebush
Any loaded or unloaded gun became a dud fluorescent tube
Some mushrooms are alphabetical some are tied with string
The moustache hides the kangaroo's resemblance to Virgil
An emu wouldn't hide it but then an emu wouldn't have it
They are both adept at taking down corrupt police in public
Making gentrified settlement look like a two-bit movie set
With a pothole wet enough to bog a duck despite drought

Who will we talk about?   A watermelon that tells time?
That wears cherries for hands that bring laughter and joy
Laughter and youth to the melon but also to its pilgrims
Seekers of time from the modern streets of New Holland
That will never be as modern as the original Holland
Because its capitalism's so poorly integrated into the beach
Which is why Canberra will never understand Sydney
Narrow crowded Sydney where a watermelon can't roll
While Canberra is designed to exemplify a big watermelon
A watermelon that can kick goals for aspirations no one has
A watermelon looks at its watch on a train in Perth or Sydney
Or Newcastle which even has a watermelon football league

Who will we talk about?   The girl with the button eye?
When she tied herself to a sunset it looked like she could fly
Her father was the tailor he sold black market cigarettes
Everyone wanted to marry her knowing that she'd inherit
They wrote and scratched her name until it covered the town
So she changed it and buttoned herself to the next train out
She got a job in the city buttoning votes for a useless mayor
When the campaign was over she fixed everything herself
One hot afternoon she lay with her eye buttoned to the creek
Smoking something special that her father had sent her
Dissatisfaction began to fasten itself to her dry inner eye
She realised that the city completely lacked concrete poetry

Who will we talk about?   A wombat smarter than Croesus?
Believe it this wombat lived in a burrow lined with books
Putting no limit on reading they sometimes stretched the day
Everyone around thought the day seemed longer than usual
So they ate more pie or sheared more sheep or watched TV
The wombat mostly read but sometimes wrote in a diary
Their ancestors had once harboured some white criminals
Whose bags of banknotes were still hidden behind a shelf
The money the wombat knew was of great historical value
But nothing to the broader history of the earth and suffering
In the sky was a constellation resembling a reading wombat
And in the morning on the ground there arrived a fresh book

Who will we talk about?   The coffin with legs that walked?
For some reason they were always talked about as if a man
Like they were a figure of death rather than an effect of it
Yet he was always welcomed and helped people laugh again
He had a lot of stories about being found asleep in the bush
Or in someone's front yard and folk would try to bury him
Yes it's good to get warmed up and remember coffin man!
Sometimes people would try to open his lid and feed him
He wasn't a living body in a coffin the coffin was his body
Yet it changed with the seasons and with his mise en scène
He never wanted people to feel uncomfortable seeing him
Only at art museums would he risk a bit of expressionism

Who will we talk about?   The magpie that was a cop?
Yeah just thinking about supplementary legs reminds me
That magpie had legs that looked extendable like a crane's
It spent a lot of time getting drunk and shooting off ammo
That's the kind of expendable member of the force they like
Feathers will fly detached from its body before story ends
Your stories always tend toward the violent I've noticed
Not anyone can be sure of a safe life especially in a colony
A crane won't swoop down and save a cabbage from moths
What did the magpie say when it was mocked for its job?
Better a magpie cop than a seagull waiter or starling actor
That always makes me laugh and feel better about the law

Who will we talk about?   The childless crying rabbit?
Unable to have kittens the rabbit cried a river and an ocean
The salty deluge flowed to a nearby farm reaching a lamb
The lamb was newly orphaned and shrank in the rising water
Then lost its footing till it floated to the burrow of the rabbit
Some say the rabbit was childless because it was a buck
Some say the rabbit was childless because it was a virgin
The rabbit stopped crying at the sight of the tiny baby sheep
There was still the problem of the tears what would they do?
They added colour to it to make paint and dirt to make clay
They say the rabbit's burrow is the oldest avant-garde cave
In the country and all agree that the wool works are marvels

Fiat In Turin

The engines are revving for the flowering of Spring

We've gone inside with the bluebells, literary bluebells
naturally. I am in your shirt pocket, where I always
wanted to be. New Order plays somewhere outside but
it's borderline dance music for me, and I freeze and –
from inside your pocket – put the water in with the tea

And what the lover did to the mower, I do to Fiat's
workers in Turin

Perhaps however that's another me, another blow-in
consultant, another bird on another wind. Two of us
playing discus, eating biscuits, a musical two obviously

And what Fiat in Turin did to its workers, you do to my
thoughts and me

Inside the yard but outside Italy. Grass tips in your hair
like a mower's 'Bohemian Rhapsody' under the noise, as
dandelion and co appear to be destroyed. Haha laughs a
fictional rat, did you get that? Like a poet need record an
execution for a general reader's thrills. Two of us in the
mailbox getting snailed on. Not the same two, logically

And what grass seeds did to the mower's lungs I do to the
workers of Fiat in Turin

Poems go into and out of minds. Think of Tennyson in
the mind of Roger Casement. Think of the same poem in
the mind of Queen Victoria at the same time. Two of us
in the basement but never mind that. Superfluous rhymes
were a thing of the time. Critics disagree on Wordsworth
all the time. I spend my time looking for someone while
at home, while someone else is looking for home. They
could be on their way there. Lighten up. The Fiat workers
will all be dead soon. The factory managers too. Shine a
light on the way terrorism was used as an excuse to
dismantle a workforce. Two of us printing t-shirts. Think
of John Lennon living long enough to read Simon Jarvis

And what the mower did to the dandelion and the
dandelion's friends, I do to the thoughts of the Fiat
workers in Turin

Or to listen to New Order, collaborate with New Order or
read Ricks on Larkin in the *New York Review of Books*
He did live long enough for that but who knows, did he?

What Stevie Smith did for waving, what Fiat in Turin did
for Italian workplace relations, what Juliana did for the
mower and his thoughts, for Marvell and his peaceful
oblivion, you, and the light of the future which no shade
can hope to alleviate, do to the two of us, and to union bust
to me

Family Trees

Ash begat Maud begat Nora begat Cicely begat Toffee
begat Toula

Wattle begat Scissors begat Freckle begat Sunny begat Carol
begat Brenda

Apple begat Susan begat Tracey begat Laura begat Gwenda
begat Sorrel

Peaches begat Sandy begat Triple Choc begat Tanya begat Twisty
begat Rose

Box begat Wafer begat Delightful begat Chewy begat Cuddles
begat Jewel

Shady begat Parakeet begat Tulip begat Rhoda begat Homily
begat Sneeze

Willow begat Norma begat Lolly begat Hannah begat Velvet
begat Louise

Silky begat Golly begat Petal begat Snooker begat Runner
begat Beans

Poplar begat Missy begat Snoopy begat Euchre begat Poker
begat Jean

Olive begat Mandy begat Fury begat Patches begat Chess
begat Queen

Heaven begat Bee begat Honey begat Leopard begat Possum
begat Coal

Blossom begat Lacy begat Useless begat Fairy begat Pamela
begat Peas

Quince begat Berry begat Trudy begat Siobhan begat Cruz
begat Mia

Cypress begat Fern begat Pearl begat Mist begat Ivy
begat Pez

Sycamore begat Camel begat Oasis begat Strings begat Glory
begat Camille

Chestnut begat Smoky begat Blur begat Snood begat Goldy
begat Jackie

Lemon begat Red begat Kelly begat Lotus begat Sky
begat Rain

Monkey Puzzle begat Crackers begat Snooze begat Dreamy
begat Dell begat Bell

Defeat Of Pitt

Even a tragedy has to start somewhere: a time, a place, an
agreement or assumption that the hero's fall makes sense

It's not yesterday or there'd be no fly buzzing around the
room. I hope it's not tomorrow just yet. A line for the writ-
er, a line for the reader. It's only fair. Pitt will be defeated
Pitt's the good one, in his blue jumper. Not Mike in a yell-
ow suit – nor Cherry the 'Kiama Scammer' in her green

Mike never took his punishment, nor his drink out of his eye-
sight. He wasn't good-looking like Pitt, who trees would
walk off with. Pitt blowing bubbles for the homeless, what
a character, playing canasta with the widows. Hurt in love
all men were hurt in love, often by themselves. Mike check-
ing his investment portfolio like a lily pond in an iPhone
holder. Cherry pushing to the front of the queue on a hot
day to buy all the frozen yoghurt. Then just dumping it out-
side a school or a cats' home. Those two were going places

They were on fire, not like Pitt who would one day look back
on his days running the environment raffle as a high point

Mike and Cherry were pulled towards Pitt, but wanted to
bring him down. Better a fly in the ointment than two in
the food. A line for the reader. A fly buzzing in an ear

Pitt so unphotogenic yet so adorable in written description
the opposite of a charismatic leader: so the past, like his
neck. I can't begin to tell you all the things I've left out
Don't let me write anyone into a corner. Mike and Cherry
at opposite cafes, crying into any dry lap they can find, a-
bout Pitt

Dear Pop

Everything we do and say in patriarchy can be traced
back to 'Strangers In The Night'. Your faded jeans, my
faint daytime smile. (Dazzling's so expensive.) Bad
Mailer novels; lose-money-quick schemes. A fortune in
friendship, nevertheless. Beef farmers favour self-flesh
awareness. (Or brittle in toffee queen regimes.) Thoughts
as feats of strength. The figure in the woodpile as a
white snake, two needle bites. The end of the week, of
us, strangers now or not? I'm dressed in white, I am the
right blonde in the wrong seaplane, I haven't learnt the

language yet. The meta-leopards will have taken over
the aquarium. They'll stroll this way like kangaroos to
green glass. Papa, I've upset you. There'll be a line of
songs like crystals lining up to kiss the bell that says Big
Town. We are on the roof now, playing to Central Park
everyone hot in their coats. Paid for not stolen. They
admit to being too late for miracles, for charity. The
poem's parents are in the front row. The poem's friend
interprets. Can we repeat it without going back to the
start, the lover's demand like ants beneath the plaint?

In Eden, in Athens, estrangement flowers. We turn and
return. Is it love itself, beckoning from the lurid grass-
lands? There's a cuteness to plaster's novelty hiding of
the body. People are cited in the mouth, stand on the

ground. They fly like Lucy. You can deny it all for fun
and parties, as if the mind was the feeling that input
gives. It's a power no one likes to admit, as it so often
leads to failure in later life, like living in a swimming
pool, or losing your tongue in the mail. What of
romances with characters from books? Alice says hello

I remind her of a cookie in a dream she had of heaven or
hell – but which was it? Everything that happens in the
world has someone to say it's their fault, repress it as
they may. The cutout in the cocktail bar wants to go
home with someone for once. The snakeskin hangs on
the gate like it's a street corner, that each uttered 'baby'
renews. Knowing can be a means to forgetting, also
We stand there as if the floor or wall is our companion
our fortress in trouble: mates a bit longer, keeping sex at
bay. Not everyone looks where they're going or cares

where others are. They're the rugged ones, though fleet
as moths when crossing a highway. Sometimes, despite
our own egos, we admire this, as if wise that the pattern
of the one ahead won't ultimately save or brave us
Don't rush. The star we wake to mightn't always be
there, so we wander outside as if air were itself a prayer
or someone's. Is that for me? addressing an ivy or a wet
plank, suddenly hungry. Tell me what happened to Peter
and Wendy and the loser with the hook for a hand. Was
it all alright in the end? They say time is nothing but it

takes the saying to make it so. To be the one is to
vanquish Sinatra, but also life (not that life is patriarchy)
Repress the possibility for the sake of staying young, as
around the bend a boat may contain the set of problems
that will have always been around. Attitudes to dancing
housework, contraception, ever music's themes. A wall-
flower may remind themselves of wallpaper, peeling to
reveal a peasant who goes to sleep at dusk behind their
tux, but does that haunt you more than the possibility
of possessing truth? Is that what your glances are about?

Care Continuum

Nothing is too small for your embrace
Or tall: the blue-green leaves of the gums
that need no names, as their scent falls
in banks of air we can almost hear the
sugar ants; spiders swing like Tarzans

A man with a sad face, a woman liable
to fall sideways at any expression of
affection. A boss, a mother, subject
to community pressure: exacerbating
the worst parts of their personalities

Close your eyes, and watch a crane
land. Think of someone watching
children with no bad intentions, as if
they're magnified snowflakes or
battery-operated razorblades. Make

cakes in the shape of favourite islands
for the geography lesson. The black-
board says things about you that aren't
true or fair. You have a stripe in your
hair from the psychiatric treatment

In the yam garden, among the mulch
there's a general rustling narrative. The

birds get distracted by their audience and
forget to play their assigned parts. The
woman has a school friend who's skilled

at flower arranging. The boss knows how
to let you down fast after years of dangling
The relief of the final spoiling, of the loved
thing. You retrieve it from the bin as if
shame is merely a function of time. It is

It's not safe to have a pet in this place
(unless you pick one mouse, and let
each mouse be the one). In the yam
garden, in the dollhouse, where if you
look close you'll see the torn pages of

a story, about a mother under an earlier
kind of pressure to give up, and who
is now just a character. There will be
joy in the dust, and the laugh of a boy
with blue hair who brings a bottle of

chardonnay (he thought it was chablis)
There was a family that drove to the beach
to get away from the police, but the people
they shared the sea with were worse than
what they'd escaped. They are serving some-

thing in the dollhouse, cups of glue with burnt
matches. Word gets around, I have a kind
of chemical imbalance, and unpaid library
fines. I didn't want to rush the books, to
startle the lines with my blonde eyes. We

know a workplace can be the setting for
all kinds of emotions, and that to think
about the ethics of different acts is a kind
of shirking. I do things with the bodies
of colleagues or strangers I can't bear

to do with my own. Everyone has a right
to hate springtime, or to bleed from their
caffeine addiction. If I don't read I float
away. You look at me and kiss me on Sydney
Road, or behind a hedge in Exhibition

Gardens. This is barely the beginning
There is so much talking to do, at the rate
of one word a day, slowly increasing, and
beyond the little things that fall from trees
but are themselves trees, inscribed with falling

Black Coffin With Milk

Take the measure of wooden speech with a wooden tongue
The sound waves crash in, like a handful of grasshoppers
Take the nails and bang them into the weeping painting
The kids are shouting what they're for: it's making noise
Making noise and drinking milk with a magnifying glass

The ancestor's dead from reading books and breathing
From boxing vegetables and reading books and breathing
The cardboard boxes are in his brain in tiny mirroring bits
From the vein in his forehead to the vein in his toe they run
They run like children to the school milk and the myths

Out of the crush they would say of him, mad as a string
The trees would say different phrases when they saw him
Out of grace, they never were, they would mimic Umback
The leaves in his hair were the marks of a bush comedy
A bush comedy so good it could run forever without seats

The little version of the novel, every novel he read at night
That he played out with his bosses, with strangers, his wife
The wife has another ancestor with the same name, related
That the lightning spilled down the hill in hot liquid form
A form that was repeated and parodied in the hill's plants

Take this string and wrap it round the painting as if alive
As if alive and attempting to survive out there in the bush
Take the clock and time the boy who went to get the milk
As if you can get milk from a large white rabbit that makes
The sound of death, chewing grasshoppers like a machine

Avec Merci

It's not as simple as saying what you see
I've seen things I haven't looked at. But
I've looked at things too, their light
streaming over me. Our quick emotions
live on the surface of our body. We can
feel delight, even love in the sight of an
object. When we look at things for a long
time, when we feel we have really seen it
that's when seemingly, a conduit opens
along a line – of light if you like – a
conduit of something that's almost
sorrow, a feeling of mercy. Mercy in a
fourth floor flat … I can see the joke in
that: of looking at a pot plant and having
a spiritual experience. So perhaps now
that I've said what I've seen, I will
digress towards the unseen. I walk into
the sedge with a mirror, alive as a weed

It looks like it hasn't heard a joke in a
while. The African boxthorn has escaped
I whisper, and Keats is dead. What has
been said and what goes unsaid? The
writing's on the water you could say, the
corn has withered on the stalk, and I
would add old friend, you aren't my
brother. In all mercy I've three already

You have found yourself in the wrong
colony. But come with me, I've left all
my ex-lovers logically enough, they
should be harmless. Let me show you a
portrait: there they are, vibrant as
African boxthorn, even in a mirror. But
they are all light like you. They are
sensible. You can't make a living from
sedge, so drain the marsh and see. The
painting is something of an oracle
whispering to me. What good is a mirror
then? A mirror's a reminder, of things
being seen, of unalive being. My hands
scribe words as if they don't know them

Where would I be if I started feeling
mercy towards them? It's the saying that
seems to come from somewhere else
the air maybe. Words will not drain me
if I look pale it's just the sunlight

Everything I do I do in the mirror
everything I see I see twice. Is that not
you my knight, shimmering in the glass
like a vertical horizon? Coming out of
my side like an unwiped stripe of paint?

What we say and see may reveal our
complexes and obsessions, despite
refusals to live in our own century, but
the way complaints become words or
even ours (having long lain down in the
dust in our quiet blood's rhythm, in the
midsummer light, and given our
thoughts up to boasting memory) is still
I would say, inevitably ghosting a lie or
a mystery – from the herb garden to the
hawthorn tree – that is as far as I can see

As If Writing A Poem

As if oats were hand rolled by elves out of Milton, or
Donne. As if gods made reports by dropping a marble or
pigeon egg from the tops of tall buildings, as if this was
somehow poetic, as if poems could be written at such
heights and yet be flimsy, amateurish, economy-righting (as
if they knew anything about that), as if businesspersons
could make concrete their decisions, that would be

remembered as images by children walking through Bourke
St Mall, as if this act had the least trace of fart or peacock
feather in it. As if with pen or keyboard, throwing dice
under the feet of Moses. As if welcoming a reader, speaking
with a voice of ivy entwined with mesquite. As if by
rhyming or making a salient metaphor, you bring into
visibility each bird of prey, lined up as an infinite target. As

if rewriting a ballad with gold ink and giving it to a servant
to deliver on a brumby. As if holding a mic close to a mouse-
trap all night. As if standing immobilised with a notebook
en route to the john. As if juxtaposing writing in native
violet icing, with knitting mittens (for a spearmint-coloured
kitten on Oscar Wilde's birthday, and naming it Speranza
after his mother). As if using a wallaby track to find a stolen

iPad. As if singing up storms of lopped white hydrangeas
like it was the French Revolution – or an opera based on
anecdotes from it. As if blank paper curled in wire made
more sense marked with rust. As if black pepper, as if
eating related to the phrases of Sappho. As if repetition was
language itself calling out to the shepherds who work land-
mined fields. As if fireworks have courage or empathy

Apple Tree

It has no idea what beauty is, till its first blossom
time. And each reminder's only a faint slide. This is
the voice of the apple tree, it sorrows as it loses its
leaves, it triumphs when laden with red or green fruit
An apple tree is no brute

but a complex of echo and self-regard. Oh, it does not
understand the agony of seasons: it lives. Its voice has
no sound yet falls pinky white. I want to fall like apple
blossom in the hair of the wrong guy, make a place for
his footsteps. Go on, bruise yourselves

children I will say. Spring looks like a bridal time but
an apple tree has no need of betrothal. Call the fire
brigade, call the ski lift: it's just the weather of the apple
whose leaves make little impress among the detritus of
autumn. Sweep a broom for appearance's sake

André Gide And The Honey Sandwich

It was in the Parc Monceau or the Jardin des Plantes (or was it both?) that my father had encountered André Gide. 'Our encounter' was what he called it. He couldn't however, remember a thing that Gide had said, and disappointingly refused to fabricate. 'Didn't he at least lay a hand on your leg?' my grandmother would ask in sarcastic umbrage, as if her Willie wasn't cute enough. 'I stalked him, I guess you would say, in today's parlance,' said my father uncertainly. All his life – and this tendency infected the whole family – flowers would remind him of childhood, of wandering around with his finger in a novel, and, naturally, of Gide. 'Oh' we would say, as we walked along a country town street, seeing a lilac bush ahead, 'I feel a reminiscence of when young'. We liked to adopt this fake way of speaking when with third parties to test their mettle. 'Gide,' my brother would say, 'was like an avocado, hiding on a footpath.' I would nod, 'Yes, you have it exactly, Otto!' 'Why are you talking about Gide?' our acquaintance would ask, feigning mildness. 'Oh, it's an old family story. There's even a song about it: Father, Father was so fair, he was too fair for André.' I would move my head as if familiar with the tune. 'But aren't you all just Anglo Celtic farming stock, that came on a boat half-chained?' Acquaintance is a cruel relation: it's better to stick with family, and the odd French novelist, or person of letters. If only our father had had the internet, how much more Parisian he could have been. 'Gide,' my brother would remark, 'once wrote a short novel on the feeling of pushing an acquaintance into a holly, just for the sake of it.' Our mother was really no better, having married our father with no illusions but the ones they admired in each other. She was often in bed, Colletting. It was no vain exercise either: she wrote most of her stories there. I would bring her coffee, sometimes three times an hour, affecting vagueness. She never refused it, but sometimes it went on the maidenhair. I claimed to recognise the rhythm of my presence in the appearance of lovers in her writing. My grandmother was tolerant but too active for genuine involvement in the family mystique. She would stand at the fire, give a report on so-and-so at church or the market, and be off again. She had, no doubt all kinds of interactions that could be turned to anecdotes; unlike the rest of us who tended to repeat the same notes in different styles. But she preferred to list facts. 'So-and-so had a red jumper on and a black eye': that sort of thing. Our parents liked to pretend that theirs was a marriage of convenience, much like mine and Otto's claims to be adopted, or the progeny of an attractive lodger, when we were eight. 'We don't have violet eyes, like father.' Everything about father was either violet or related to Elizabeth Taylor in some way. Our sister Erica once told an uncaring cousin that André Gide was the name of a horse in a

Taylor vehicle. We always called movies vehicles. 'Are you going to that Streep vehicle?' our mother would call, hearing us lifting our coats from the rack in the hall. 'I've made you all violet sandwiches for lunch,' Erica would threaten. More of an artist than a fabulator, she would spend hours draping bread and butter with mushrooms, olives, and the skins of eggplants, trying to get an effective hue. It was this sandwich venture that prompted another miniature memory in our father. Yes, I brought them with me to tempt him, he said. He had given a honey sandwich to the tired writer, who he came across resting on a bench, staring at the follies in the Parc Monceau. 'The sandwiches come to the old bird,' Gide had said to the fair young boy with the red nose. 'This fable serves to prove, that those who are already sweet need no vehicles,' said my brother, who was considered the wise one of the family. The old bird had whistled for a carriage, apparently drawn by a velvet horse, and ridden off among the pyramids. We were satisfied. We would finally move on to something respectably Anglo Celtic. Or begin wearing mascara mos like parody Mona Lizes

Adjectival Or The English Canon

The following history isn't particularly edifying or pretty
Depending on perspective if floating high above the action
Popping eyes running veins might appear effusions of life

To be martyred for poetry is the highest a poet can aspire
Agnostic or Catholic whether inclined to think that canons
Metaphorically or literally substitute for afterlives Greek

Or Biblically stratified all aim ultimately to be crucified
Which shouldn't be so hard to achieve except for this rub
Each candidate for godhead must attract a worthy assassin

Earliest details are patchy the lists could still be shaken up
By the discovery of new archives or mass graves to excite
The industry and literary types who love a lurid biography

But I must get on or impatient readers will turn to TV
Which churns even Persia and Scotland into plot and talk
Our lineup begins with a well-known droll Canterburian

First English poet-cum-deity aka Bloody Geoffrey Chaucer
Reckon some quasi-French proto-troubadour took offence
Beat his head with a pike yet local spoken worder as likely

Bloody Thomas Wyatt had not been born so he'd no boast
Yet somebody thought his verse worth exalting post-breath
Probably Henry VIII he adored his wives' poems to death

Poetic murder mystery populariser Bloody John Skelton
He got the whole court intrigued including Philip Sidney
Philip invited John to his stables then had its roof collapse

He might've made a career of it if his life had stretched a bit
But was still perfecting his tale of the squashing of JS when
Accidentally suffocated at a house party playing sardines

Bloody Edmund Spenser would've had and enjoyed the job
Possibly his Faerie Queene even suggested it one tête-à-tête
Walter Raleigh sent him a get well spud in the mail from jail

Raleigh was the next to go from a bad head cold so I'm told
The royal cats loved Sir Walt sang along in his demise song
Bloody Thomas Campion bored the cats but who killed him?

Fulke Greville the gay baron according to servant gossip
Astrologically blessed in his birthdate he can wear the debit
Strong opponent of marriage by royal poets he died of a flu

Christopher Marlowe was a cute and early adaptor of TB
Shakespeare would have done him in given half a chance
No apotheosis for Marlowe though a credible angel I wen

Bloody William Shakespeare got the whole world into verse
Eventually had his throat cut by Bloody Benjamin Jonson
Jonson then proclaimed Shakespeare's spirit'd entered him

Bloody John Donne did for Ben of course as is well-known
Strung a wire by his lane one night when Jonson was drunk
Half took his head off Donne was said to regret the bad job

Bloody George Herbert as he was known from then on
Treacherously invited Donne to a Haymarket intersection
With a prod of the cane into traffic he never breathed again

A tough assignment Bloody John Milton confided in writing
Squashing Herbert like a flea or jonquil with a stone mallet
That is the irony of the times and of being Milton he thought

Bloody Andy Marvell my favourite of the whole bloody lot
Was well-named and could've taken out Wimbledon also
He put JM among the stars after Charles II put out his eyes

Marvell killed with a pillow but no decorous death for him
Bloody John Wilmot preferred a dramatically bloody show
Predictably mowing Marvell to death Juliana was suspected

Wilmot aka Rochester was known for his aversion to labour
Also for his taste in German shepherds but that is by the by
Bloody John Dryden poisoned him with cyanide in his rye

Make me godly but not yet Bloody William Cowper he said
Cowper put a hole in Dryden's dinghy one fatal hot summer
Bummer said he who'd had no anxiety about its eventuality

Bloody Alex Pope rather revelled in booting Bill Cowper
Off his mortal coil and into the literary history curriculum
Apotheosis for that religious ninny local pub critics scoffed

A bloody boy did for Pope by choking him with a bell rope
Bloody Thomas Chatterton was well keen on this canon lark
Strung him up to test his prosody up close and farkin' far up

Lucky he didn't get splattered by Pope which wouldn't count
Doubted Bloody Christopher Smart was clearheaded enough
Called on the pantheon for action got an arrow in the throat

Bloody Thomas Gray offed Smart on a daring impulse
Dropping around with a new ode he found him in his bath
CS was found there later fully clothed stone cold beaming

Gray like most poets a slippery character ate his own razor
Bloody Samuel Johnson wrote all about it in an exposé
Lives of the Poets was Agatha Christie's bedtime reading

Johnson famous for the remark after me the dribble waited
Bloody William Blake set fire to Johnson in the main street
TIGER BURNS BRIGHT WRITER as one headline cried

So much for the dribble eh Johnson Blake would mutter
Indeed reiterated Bloody William Wordsworth utter chaff
WW invited Blake to a picnic and Blake stumbled off a cliff

While William got the credit some say that Dorothy did it
Dorothy liked to quote Lady Macbeth casually to guests
Bloody Samuel T Coleridge finally taking her broad hint

Planning it all in the lime tree bower one broody afternoon
Dropped a rock on W's head how sublime! they both said
Bloody George Lord Byron gave Coleridge a rabbit-chop

So many men to kill so few centuries you might well think
There's more to go too like Bloody Percy Bysshe Shelley e.g.
Shelley didn't believe in this divine poet malarkey of course

Yet Bloody Byron did get on his nerves from time to time
Rabbiting on about honour etc. Shelley took his breastplate
Thinking to decorate the ship's cabin then drowned at sea

Bloody John Clare was not mad but rather a time traveller
He was a wizard with a long scarf he'd knitted himself
Conjuring winds he sank Shelley's ship from the madhouse

Bloody John Keats was at a loss spending many days loafing
Thinking about how to revenge Percy and become a god too
Finally he wrote to Clare enclosing a coughed-on hanky

Who would be fated to end the pain of the sparrow Keats?
Who else but Bloody Emily Brontë clomping on a walk
Of all the killings in this history perhaps the kindest meant

Bloody Thomas Lovell Beddoes staged a makeshift tragedy
Polonius to her Hamlet he stabbed her from behind a blind
Charlotte was impressed by Emily's realistic death scene

Seizing her chance Bloody Elizabeth Bloody B Browning
Dripped her way into the canon with TLB's severed head
Robert wasn't impressed with what that did to the carpet

Statistically it's likely he had something to do with her death
Officially it was Bloody Dante Bloody G B Rossetti who
Filled her cloak hood with bees on learning of her allergies

Poignantly Rossetti himself died of chalk dust asphyxiation
Bloody Matthew Arnold made him write out a million times
I must not murder poets on a bet not even while in Italy

Imagine how his wrist ached and imagine Arnold's own end
Apparently done in by Bloody Gerard Manley Hopkins
Death by anchor while minding his own business on a beach

Hopkins heaved it at him in a vision of Arnold as Antichrist
That's what the *Daily Mail* said eight years later anyway
Bloody Christina Rossetti made a special trip to Dublin

Putting paid to the morbid nun appreciator with a cricket bat
Upside GMH's head and she might've been on the pitch still
If Bloody Robert Browning hadn't shot her to join the game

He wanted to be last for the century to be the Browning era
He'd forgotten the Bloody White Rabbit late to the party
Smothered by fur in the afternoon sun he never woke up

Charles L Dodgson better known as Bloody Lewis Carroll
Dead of exhaustion running late for the Pantheon 9.05
Bloody Algernon Swinburne driving a deadly brakeless train

His own death inaugurating the bloody twentieth century
We've heard too much of it picture adjectival Wilfred Owen
Bona fide snuffer out of Germans in a field of bloody poets

Acts

Unemployed man writes poem in one room slab hut
Mother, sister, cop, gunshot. Brother: absent, blamed
Moon turns black-eyed face away, roses wilt
Currawong forgets its name: calls duck, pigeon

Unemployment gang. Lost, reckless children range
Dresses worn for shame (dresses suiting eucalypts)
Moon hops in hope of losing hunters. Cops die on
duty, pensions paid. The Survivor wins the Cup

Poem 'Mosquitoes should be left in peace' wins pub
slam. No other entries allowed on fear of crop death
Moon's face on wanted poster. Honey for sale sign
by burrow. Koala on chain gang for peppermint theft

Unemployed poet wears tracking device in bush
Moon mistaken for helicopter: shot down. Rust
sweeps through prisons. Bars, locks, guns crumble
Escapees eat roses right off bushes, get shot at

Currawong writes poem, signs it The Kookaburra
Mother and sister hop sideways to evade cops
Poodle blamed. Wombat mistaken for bonsai hedge
Poem goes unpublished, poet wears oil drum in rain

Brother and friends die on job, no regrets. Moonlight-
in-water-eating-carp sink to bottom. Feral cats roam
state. Raid farms, traverse rivers, borders like birds
Honey trap for hunting party too rough to resist

Abstraction

Tune in to the valley, the blue tree – chords fly up
        into its cardboard branches

These things had been real just a moment ago, but
now we were feeling something different

Delicious like an afternoon onion, autumn's onion

The blue skin between the teeth, my tooth had been
real and now it hurt: it hung from a faded surfer's
shirt

        It fell out in the fruit of a dangerous noon
while everything was ripening slowly in the cool

        A palm fell across the road, and the shadow
        of the tree fell on the beach and spread
towards the gold coast customs

Water fell out of the leaves and into a machine
        and the conversation became a cutout

We were wearing suits and you said that you felt
primitive, reading an old book with x-ray vision

That was what the Romantics did in stormy weather
        and made hay

And made hay and listened to God on the
radio, because the waves were stronger then

There was nothing to take the weight of the cove

The heavy sun

An old camel with a star on its back, parked
behind a tea factory, the guards playing two-up
and listening to ABBA like it was Christmas

I brought you a sundae, but somehow the
cherry fell off and that was the end of trust between
us, and between me and the road quite
frankly

Chunks of ice in the apple, a way of seeing the
world that made others back away, smiling and
tilting their heads

Sydney became based there like an experiment of
doubling, and it became fascinated with its own
bays and was like to fall in, drowning its libraries
their barrowfuls of dictionaries

I camped underneath a statue of Henry
Lawson, and noted how its head bifurcated the sky
and did not think it a coincidence

A movie started playing, and we asked if we
had caused this?

We're so used to it, we would think everything was
a cheap set if we went back to the past

There are so many countries in the northern
hemisphere that they spend all their time counting
them, and putting the numbers in books and saying
of the books, look how many countries are in
the books

An emu is shying around the pavlova: how did
it get there and when?

We dressed in cameras from that moment on

A long letter came on ship for the governor
but it got wet and some tore off, or was eaten by a
dog and anyway it was only orders on how to run
the country, and what styles of painting to
encourage and how to manipulate dinner
parties, and very tonally off-putting too

The governor decided to quarantine the ship

Yet when he woke up there were traces of blue ink
on his face, or else his veins had come up out

of his cheeks and nose and tongue, and they
photographed him like that and the newspapers said
this is how we must live

We make a dirty joke and look up at the moon
blacked out by peacocks flying in from the tea
factory, and we think of the pools of boiling water
awaiting them

Do you have a knife?

It has a wooden blade and a metal handle
and it sits in the museum like this

Each idea different from the last, each
dancer straining to understand what it meant to be
between gravity and the land, the gravity wanting to
get to the next planet

The poem was similar to one from Japan without
the same import, or ending

A peacock proud of its shirt, stolen from a
line

The shutters blocked out some of the noise from the
government messengers, yet also misdirected our
Valentines

Everything that had seemed to turn on a pin
reflected another pin somewhere else, and when the
neighbours began to complain about the possums, I
put my head into the mailbox and kept it there

When they died, the they that used to be us, and our
survivors went through our hard drives and
everything else for a greater sense of what
we had been, there were many tantalising clues and
skeletons of tiny creatures that might have been our
avatars but the expense of forensics was
prohibitive, so mostly they surmised we had been
born in a game and had more or less stayed near
each other, fabricating a long exchange that
might or might not have been useful for them, if
knowledge had stayed the same a bit longer

In the garden a kind of play

In the palm tree a kind of bear

A bear whose image adorned a petrol station
or donut franchise, but had never been real
and perhaps served as the double for
someone else who hadn't been either

The emu pecking on the piano a song that meant as
bad as it sounded, that troopers were on the way, that
the squatter was collecting rents

We divided up some of the pretexts for the
beginning of the world, and sold some and sewed
some into our pockets and carefully hit the road

We divided up too, some of the pretexts for the
        ending of the world and sold some, and
chewed some into tiny bits of tobacco, and carefully
hit the sky rending the clouds on our way through

GRASSLANDS

FENCELANDS

Greta And The Cream

Greta watered the succulents with an old Voss bottle she had picked up at an airport. She thought of the man she'd met in the cafe, while waiting for a delayed flight. He was Russian – spoke Spanish and English – and in fact translated Latin American authors into Russian. He talked about his holiday, he had been in Dublin for the first time, and coincidentally had met another Australian there, a psychologist called Shawn. Shawn was interested in Russian fiction, Latin American fiction, and after midnight in The Black Door, would tell Pyotr the plots of the novels he'd read. Pyotr of course knew his national classics, but didn't read contemporary novels. The books he translated were generally related to music and dance. He doubted sometimes whether Shawn was relating the narratives from memory or making them up. There was one about two sisters in love with the same man; eventually the man leaves town. Later he finds out they're raising a child together but they refuse to tell him which of them is the mother. He leaves his son from another relationship with them overnight and then falls into a ravine. Pyotr had said to Greta that he had the insight, that's the word he'd used, that there might be a national, or at least cultural, way of reading stories that made everything you read – or at least everything you remembered, that meant something to you – a story from your culture. Greta said, perhaps you heard the stories as Australian because Shawn was telling them. But what she guessed – and she assumed Pyotr had considered this possibility also – was that what Shawn was actually doing was fictionalising the stories of his patients, relieving the pressure of keeping them secret, but without – technically – breaking confidentiality. Shawn had been an only child and had, he told Pyotr, staged performances for his parents, of the psychoanalysis of his toys and the family cats, doing all the voices himself. Shawn told him that he had once reduced his parents to tears telling the pathetic story of a kitten left at the tip. Pyotr admitted that Shawn had a mesmerising tone, and had thought at the time that Shawn could probably get him to do anything – like buy all the drinks – simply by asking him to do so. As Greta remembered it (or was that because of an email Pyotr had sent later?) the holiday seemed to go on for years, with Shawn beginning to repeat the stories, about finding his father in the ravine, and the crows telling him to say nothing; and when he went back the next day there was no body, just a chess set on a rock, and an instruction to close his eyes for one minute between each move. Cannily, the pieces on the board would move in that time, and it seemed likely that he was playing the crows. Greta drank from the Voss bottle, feeling upset by the memories but unsure why. She had left the cream on the table and her cat Fargo was guarding it. 'It's just you and me, kiddo' she said. 'No one else wants it.'

Despite being emotional, just as Pyotr had been over the days they had spent at the airport together – admittedly some of that time in bed at an airport hotel – she had felt temporarily healed, as if Shawn's effect on people, even secondhand, was therapeutic. She had imagined him asking his patients to sign releases on their stories, or a form of copyright for therapists (Pyotr had said, there was a story about why in the end Shawn had decided against psychoanalysis): that allowed them to repeat what they heard for the benefit of others only, not for profit. She had become Pyotr and Shawn, she felt. Not constantly, and perhaps not permanently, but as she read a few pages of Shklovsky aloud for its effect on Fargo, she remembered the Colombian sisters that she had met at university who said they had some kind of benefactor, which Greta had assumed then was a cover story. Well, the world was full of sisters she thought. She had one herself, who was happily married, and played in a death metal band, and voted Labor, and only read memoir, and tweeted violently all day long. She imagined that Shawn was knocking firmly at the door. She opened it calmly, cream in hand

Hamlet In The Mind Of A Country Schoolteacher

'Adani killed my father'

These words were in Adam's head when he woke up, but
he was unable to remember any dream they were part of

It was still daylight: he'd been having a nap
between class and the performance, starting at eight

He walked to the theatre, thinking about the play, went
inside: it was filthy, and a smell of gas from the
leaky radiator

He'd arrived early so he sat up the back, thinking to move
closer when others began to arrive

Hamlet's problem, he thought, was that the only truths he
had to express were ones that no one, least of all himself
wanted to hear

Last time he'd been here was for a school production of *A
Midsummer Night's Dream*; he populated the empty stage
with kids crawling over the set, and each other, in green

It emphasised an ecological theme, according to the
program, written by Nadia the drama teacher: each of the
children's different roles complemented the others'

Yet to Adam (I am an English teacher after all, he said to
himself in an aside) the children seemed more like an
alphabet than an ecosystem: forming different
letters and words as they moved across the stage, and up
and down different levels of the forest, by vine

He'd lost concentration and forgot about the plot; he was
still vague about it – unlike tonight's play, which he knew
pretty well, and which would be performed by a touring
professional company of recognisable actors

The blue shadow reminded him of his father (a ghost
rehearsing in the town theatre this bright summer evening?)

No: there was no sign of the cast; could it be gas, and in
any case his father was still alive, and not a miner
but an accountant?

What could he or Hamlet do, to stop the earth spinning to
perdition?

Pear trees grew, tree ferns too, rainforests with child-sized
snakes in them forming S's and I's and L's: be careful in
the quiet

Nadia sat next to him, but was already looking at her
phone, so he didn't zone in, only relatively, taking in his
surroundings

Yes, he had chosen the worst seat for comfort and view
so he could take that on as a martyr – he'd meant to move
but now he'd have to explain to Nadia; he was sure there
were mice droppings on the floor

He remembered being at the pub the day before, listening
to the pear farmers arguing about the Fortinbras mine, and
the likely effect on them, and their remedy for anger: a
night's spotlighting

They sounded straight out of Aristotle, or rather like the
version of catharsis argued against by Aristotle's critics

He spotted one or two of them now, looking and smelling
better than they did at the pub – except the pub was a
posher venue by far

The poster had suggested they were in for a sexy night of
TV stars half-clad and mournful, sponsored by a bank that
must be trying to look good too

The sponsorship gave Adam a bad feeling, but he thought
that on the whole, he had to side with thinking, and a play
    about thinking – however compromising the night
    or how it ended (unseasonable weather predicted)

You are the English teacher after all, as Nadia had said
    in the staffroom that afternoon

Houses

It was kind of you the lawyer said, to spare the house
when you destroyed the park. I met the lawyer at a party
I was interested in his arms; later his eyes. His name
was Lloyd he said. We were in the greenhouse, a kind
of sanctuary. It seemed endangered, it was another
house not the house I'd saved. That house had your
personality, I said in an attempt at flattery. It has my
body, Lloyd said. There have been houses in my family
for generations he supposed: I supposed he was right

It was the end of the night. A mouse somehow turned
off the light just as I was kissing Lloyd goodbye. A
magic mouse I told my mother later. She was keen on
houses, too. She would put houses in houses in houses
She lived in Tasmania because it was said there were
more houses per capita there. Per capita was a pet
phrase of my mother's. The sun shone in the window as
I was kissing her goodbye. It was unfortunate that I'd
met Lloyd just before leaving for the Northern Territory

It alarms me: the parks they have there. But I needed to
go for my research. Lloyd gave me some money and
some haute couture shirts. Say hello to Kakadu for me
he said like Kakadu was an easy going guru. Later, I
was in Central Europe and didn't see a house for many
kilometres. It seemed such a waste of space I wrote to

Lloyd in a kiosk of one of his firm's offices (they have
branches everywhere, the law was not exactly a burger
to them but a kind of cheap bread). I was taken to see a

house in the middle of the night. I wore a sequined
Warhol rip-off Liz Taylor dress. It was meant to attract
investors. They were frying fish in the yard. The street
lights made everyone's faces a kind of violet as I bent to
kiss them (I was in heels too). I realised the house didn't
belong there and had been stolen. It was like Texas all
over again, Lloyd said to me as I said it to him later
There were activists trying to destroy it. I tiptoed away
I brought home a strange kind of butterfly in my hair

Its scary markings were like the face of Brigitte Bardot
or Tomaž Šalamun (the Slovenian poet) I thought and
said to a colleague later. We had fallen out of the habit
of kissing. There was a rally to defend a house but I was
having important drinks with Lloyd. He said he would
bring me something of value, like a corporate credit card
It was a steamy night, it reminded me of stumbling over
a house in Jakarta. I was wearing sandals and a red skirt
If I was less ethical I could've put it in my pocket, I lied

If You Want To Drink Whiskey With The Big Boys You Have To Drink The Whiskey

Will it be more upsetting if I keep kissing you or if I cease?

This beauty has been
soaked in coffin wood but I
don't know whose

Are you being brutal for
appearance's sake or does it stem
from trivial motives?

If I was a woman I'd work magic with this
computer and send men running out into the streets, to
solve crimes like they're heroes

Their clothes are too good for
the work

My name is Bedingfield and I almost exist

It is wonderful to be
almost alive
wearing imaginary gloves
of human-made leather
very naturally soft

No other creature I believe, can create such leather

Knowhow might be heard as nohow

This turkey I notice has
only one eye and
one wing, like they
haven't tried out Cubism in
Kentucky – or they have and
didn't care for it: that's
perhaps as likely

Sometimes I wish I were a corrupt pope
with a gifted son, but I wake up at a
writer's festival in Europe amid gossip
about the Nobel Prize, and a rain
of kettles and saucepans so sparse
it can be dodged

What is this need to spend thousands of dollars to come to
the other side of the world to disagree with people about
literature?

Aren't there plenty
of people to
disagree with at home?

Wouldn't it better to lie alone in a studio
listening to streamed music, that costs little
or nothing?

Any kind of music, even the saddest and most
revolutionary – black tea, gypsy music – is worth five cents
to capitalism

A big stick means
nothing to me, except for
the beat it makes on my tin
chest and back and head
and legs

I went into the bank and it was
filthy with white birds which had never
been let out since the bank opened, what
kind of birds are these I asked?

Savings birds! Savings birds! the birds themselves replied

So this is what everybody
thinks about all day

This is what keeps people's blood red

The plan is for all poets to double themselves, turn up to
the party in pairs and scare the novelists (for the practice)

Our bottles are
empty, Prime
Minister we will shout, for
the party will be at the
Prime Minister's house

Then a wall will cave in, exposing the
escape plan

There are not enough wind farms in the world

To make the envelopes
marked sensitive, with
brown rings on them in
duplicate, smelling like
incense at the sweetest funeral
you've ever been to

Oh banned tubercular writer
buried at the age Bedingfield is now
sometimes when he reads, his crick-
necked lamp reminds him of you

In The Beginning Was Parody

We're heading to gentleness, the citing of violence will
then be forgotten, or seen as impolite. 'Rogues, clowns
and fools; marriage parties and dances at the house' all
doomed to the middle ages. 'Social conditions' a vast
error. Writing is everything, though many writers
disagree. We're all heading to the original
The example lies down with the parable

Rogues, clowns, and fools rule the roost, but can't write
to save a chook. We admit it's not their aim. Was the
snake in the garden real? More importantly, is footy?
Or is it a dream of fear and beauty? Rabelais says the
snake was a sausage, and might've added that sausages
play football in our insides, as we watch it on TV
The cliché lies down with hyperbole

Williams weighs a baby on a variable scale and
recommends spinach. Eventually we will live lives worth
meta-commentary, and slide into the sea, realising that
human ideas are the shapes of kelp. That chooks were
meant to be the gulls of inland: but though they watch our
best and our balls fly, they huddle to the wicket
The allusion lies down with the quote

Too much salt on spinach brings on crying: a trick used
by Greek actors, and Jacobeans in 'The Kelp Queen'
Cleopatra had a fear of being poisoned, and nibbled on the
sausage she kept in her breast. All the people she had put
to death were due to gross misreadings of games of chess
she should have been a writer of light verse
The script lies down with the chorus

Note-taking can be a job, or a job within a job. Williams
pushes his barrow of notes through Paterson, sometimes
adding a baby: to give its mother a break / time to pick
spinach. He saw social conditions everywhere he went
You're queer chooks, he said to the gulls he met. He cried
to think of all the reality we'd yet to overcome
The theme lies down with the crumb
The eye lies down with the thumb

Isaac Babel And The East Sumatran Rhino

I won't venture anything just yet I'll type my way into it
These slowly wearing keys part of extinction's trajectory
The mice-thin film of dust and oil on 'I' etcetera are mine
Drawn into a rhino-erasing epistemology not an easy word
Not a word easy to unpack or bring forth in a line of verse

There now I've five subdued lines verging on sympathy
Yesterday I found a lost painting of uncaged budgerigars
My great-grandmother painted it as an employment aside
It was a great grand day then till my taxation appointment
At least it wasn't amputation said the guy in the skate shop

He was right but I didn't ask for his thoughts on the rhino
The rhino itself competing for news space with climbers
Climbers falling like Revolution creating orphans at home
Paraphrasing Babel re orphans widows and bereaved parents
His stories make tragedy seem a rich if unwanted outcome

His own arrest torture and death no one could do justice to
If rehabilitation years later is solace then it's for his ghost
Ghosts of East Sumatran rhinos are filling a Malaysian zoo
There's not a particular point to be made here just thoughts
That converge on this year's drizzly grey last May morning

Solace is not for the dead but the living and rain the same
Snow is for the living mountain then as much as the skiers

Whether snow is for the climbers or not depends on chance
Chance or skill or concentration which writing poetry needs
But not too much as a sharp mind won't let the ghosts in

Babel's writing has been likened to a perfectly tuned guitar
Babel's ghost could slip into a zoo or strum into a jungle
To be able to write like falling snow would be a consolation
Snow seems perfect as long as not examined too closely
But that's an error snow is always perfect just as all is

Rehabilitation need be no albatross as a rhino's written
Poetry can only be solace for humans and that's its curse
When we're attuned to it it can accompany us in our grief
From grief all the way down the scale to cold feet in May
We can even ignore the vibration or ping of a message

Babel with a mobile phone would have furthered his work
His torturers and other inmates would've become characters
We would have his voice like Boochani's at writing events
That sadness which can only enrich our own or detune us
So that we fly through democracy with feathers falling out

Mixing metaphors seems like a fortuitous way to continue
Mixing realities so that one can interrupt the other's track
While poetry proceeds by figural substitution or say dance
Planting peach stones to replace asylum seekers is no go
More's the pity nor could a dead rhino take Babel's stead

Perhaps one day humans might get beyond knowing things
Further too with how other beings see our forked acts
Nonhuman beings provide solace for us but do we for them?
Lying down in the fragmented light of a peach tree to read
Looking out into bush for bilby or dingo instead of a rhino

Preoccupations in Australian fauna to adapt a Wright title
It would be solace if there were always a last Sumatran rhino
Or if the last person had been freed from torture or detention
Teapots and woomeras need a fair bit of network in between
Too late for that kitschy combination if we've lost yesterday

Tasmanian peach trees rigged up with lights for a reading
Solace my motif if it can reach a peak without weakening
I'm reading Wright's oldie 'Bullocky' to farmers and bats
Some alphabets are based on bat shapes but not the Roman
Murmurs an eccentric in a white smock there's always one

Widdershins seems like an apt place for settler thought to be
Meaning I don't know nor am I sure how anyone else could
Maybe bread making and breaking is a possible beginning
But no use to the East Sumatran rhino or Boochani or Babel
That's the living and the dead without meaning to cite White

The bread reference alludes to Pascoe's history *Dark Emu*
Solace of research and discovery and rethinking reality
Peaches are bread to bats and to farmers as poetry is to me
Peaches mixed with raw eggs saved a doctor after Hiroshima
The only thing he could swallow due to the state of his face

This is in Ibuse's novel *Black Rain* based on documents
Just one hopeful detail in a dedicated account of the bomb
The theme of my poem's not ironic despite Babel and rhino
Not merely bitterly ironic as it refers to solace as dedication
That of meaning to the meaningful in any poetic gathering

Jesus Likes Radiohead

Jesus is crawling through the desert listening to Justin Timberlake masterpieces. It is very tiring. Am I even myself? he asks. I don't even know what my favourite Donna Summer song is ('On The Radio', the same as Simon Cowell's). It is morning or evening. The stars in the sky mean nothing (no anthem writer or liar, Jesus)

He's scoring the ground with his hands and knees, it'll be a puzzle to the next pilot, who looks down and sees (perhaps a weekend musician). It's some time before he realises that Aaliyah's 'Try Again' is in his head. Jesus is no easybeat: but then he has no inkling what an easy-beat is. An unholy conjunction living for the Sabbath?

As a stab in the dark that's more or less correct. In dreams, crying is noble and nothing's lovelier than a unicorn. In reality, to cry blood is the thing. Realising that you are the hero of a life story (your own) that will be read as a pastiche of earlier figures, like Odysseus or Hercules (or even more hopeless cases, or later ones)

The ancient streets of Damascus and Jerusalem are mimicked by Ballarat's avenues. The *Saturday Night Fever* soundtrack blares from speakers for what seems like years. Or *Rumours*. He would've made for the river and dived if it wasn't for the snakes (which he believes the locals mean when they say condoms and needles)

Poor conditions are what you get when you throw in
with treacherous, weak offsiders. You share the
radiation, drink badly made tea. Best case scenario's
sitting on the side of their bed explaining why a song
which seems so sincerely romantic is narcissistic and
grim. No need to name names (pull me out of the cave)

Elvis pulls up in a truck, self-styled saviour of an hour
that's passed. (Reckons he has better tunes too.) Do they
make ears bleed Jesus asks him? Elvis's immodesty
breaks down in reply. He shyly hands the son of God a
red can of drink: colder than July. Time I went back to
headquarters. Morning arrives like the invention of neon

U U
M U U M
U M U U M U
E U M U U M U E
S E U M U U M U E S
U S E U M U U M U E S U
M U S E U M U U M U E S U M
O M U S E U M U U M U E S U M O
O O M U S E U M U U M U E S U M O O
R O O M U S E U M U U M U E S U M O O R
A R O O M U S E U M U U M U E S U M O O R A
G A R O O M U S E U M U U M U E S U M O O R A G
N G A R O O M U S E U M U U M U E S U M O O R A G N
A N G A R O O M U S E U M U U M U E S U M O O R A G N A
K A N G A R O O M U S E U M U U M U E S U M O O R A G N A K
K A N G A R O O M U S E U M U U M U E S U M O O R A G N A K
A N G A R O O M U S E U M U U M U E S U M O O R A G N A
N G A R O O M U S E U M U U M U E S U M O O R A G N
G A R O O M U S E U M U U M U E S U M O O R A G
A R O O M U S E U M U U M U E S U M O O R A
R O O M U S E U M U U M U E S U M O O R
O O M U S E U M U U M U E S U M O O
O M U S E U M U U M U E S U M O
M U S E U M U U M U E S U M
U S E U M U U M U E S U
S E U M U U M U E S
E U M U U M U E
U M U U M U
M U U M
U U

U U
MU UM
UMU UMU
EUMU UMUE
SEUMU UMUES
USEUMU UMUESU
MUSEUMU UMUESUM
OMUSEUMU UMUESUMO
OOMUSEUMU UMUESUMOO
ROOMUSEUMU UMUESUMOOR
AROOMUSEUMU UMUESUMOORA
GAROOMUSEUMU UMUESUMOORAG
NGAROOMUSEUMU UMUESUMOORAGN
ANGAROOMUSEUMU UMUESUMOORAGNA
KANGAROOMUSEUMU UMUESUMOORAGNAK
KANGAROOMUSEUMU UMUESUMOORAGNAK
ANGAROOMUSEUMU UMUESUMOORAGNA
NGAROOMUSEUMU UMUESUMOORAGN
GAROOMUSEUMU UMUESUMOORAG
AROOMUSEUMU UMUESUMOORA
ROOMUSEUMU UMUESUMOOR
OOMUSEUMU UMUESUMOO
OMUSEUMU UMUESUMO
MUSEUMU UMUESUM
USEUMU UMUESU
SEUMU UMUES
EUMU UMUE
MU UM
U U

Knitting A Poem By The Hoover Dam

Knitting a poem for Husker Du by the Hoover Dam
And other monuments. The poem looks like a bee (to
Knit Keatsianly). Knitting poems by the Harbour
Bridge, letting moisture into the wool

As it rises, as it sprays from the wake of the ferries
The life of the sea. Knitting a poem by Arthur's Seat
My Dad looking on benignly. Knitting a poem for the
Pogues at Barrowlands, and other

Bands. Knitting a poem by the Big Sheep, so waxily
Figurative, an old bad feeling creating knots and
Fissures, like some poison or prison's got in the line
Knitting a poem for my nephew, so

He might climb out of any white life that's made for
Him and his. Knitting a poem by pine trees (symbols
Of longevity) for purring black cockies to eat; or by
The great Buddha of Toganji Temple

In Motoyama. What is Bob Mould doing today
Tonight, I wonder? The knitting grows a tail like an
Unfazed gecko, becomes a poem of two tones. To
The poem the needles are home

Knitting by the Amphlett memorial in Little Bourke
Us boys desperate to get it done. Knitting to the sound
Of a gypsy band, late in the forest where gay poets
Dance, a plate of gelato and WWII

How swans make the sky look blue. The Avalanches
And Jean-Luc Godard: all get a garter. Ian Hamilton
Finlay, I've been knitting this poem all day. I'm going
To wear it at Little Sparta

Lamb To The Slaughter

Here we are again, in the church of misunderstanding, of
Landing on one less foot than we have, where
The wood is smooth like honey to the eye, like a light or so
It seems with the day lamps on. When we
Are handed a page of white paper or sail, or piece of veil

I was reading and my hope, hope or need
Was receding into barnlike comfort, but a scene appeared
Of one who wanted to learn to write through
Rhythm, something I had put aside, forgotten, forsaken to
Put it melodramatically, it wouldn't kill me

To learn to sing like sheet lightning, or cry in a new
Language like a fox, or a hybrid cheese that
Melts at the sound of Ravel. Things might change for the
Better, not at all or go to hell. Remain casual
Every possibility will occur eventually, we all need holes

To stick our heads and arms through
Mundane but only at first impression. Endless trying to. If
You can do it you don't need to, but stop and
You soon won't be able to. 'Crimson', the sentence begins
Evoking leaves of grass revisions, and ends

Liked In Prison

Walking the streets, reading his books
in the cafes and bars, this was his over-
riding question: would he be liked in
prison?

He was not particularly bad, or good, or
graceful, or skeptical. He reckoned he
belonged to the median when it came to
the smokers of Lwów: but would he be
liked in prison?

Later, he'd go home and write poems
barely thinking of the ever-more-likely
knock at the door. 'Writing poems is
like body surfing' he'd say. 'Do you
know this expression? Body surfing? I
picked it up by the Baltic Sea. You have
to ride the wave'

In the bar, this was even later, drinking –
what? Vodka, because it's transparent
or Guinness, because its transparency is
ironic? The expression, 'He (or she) can
be seen through Guinness' is one he
never knew, would never hear, even in
prison

You can star in prison and fail in
California, but who cares? Failing in
California was a fantastic dream, like
a bee drowning in Guinness, to
hyperbolise. Because the bee would
haul themselves out of the pool of
whatever alcohol in whatever bar, or
kitchen, they were in and buzz home
while the buzzing was good

A bee fails in a hive, a sparrow cries in
its tree, a poet's dragged off in the night
whether his gaolers like him might be
good, might be bad. What impression
he'll make on the other inmates is what
keeps him awake, how he'll be or seem

The effect of his voice, harsh or gentle

Long White Talksong Part One

When we first become adults we're the
perfect age to design robots. Being at
our peak of repression. A troupe of robots
are taken to Kenya, designed as white
hunters. And the grass says, we hide e-
verything, we know where everything is e-
ven the white lion. Can you see your-
selves the robots ask? The grass goes
red in the sunset. We hide our Japanese
manufacture say the robots, but only
from those who aren't trained to notice
anything. The grass revives. The robots say
where is the depot? Oh it's not far, you
will find it. They are programmed to
find it, and not programmed to worry. But
appearing needy disarms locals. And
then again, not everything is stable like
the depot, which they find has been burned
to the ground by lightning. The bank
next door and the gun shop next other
door weren't damaged. There was no grass
to ask advice. Then their depot finding
instruction changed into a garage find-
ing one. It was not a real town, but let's
say it was very much like a representa-
tion of Isiolo. The robots drive their

Toyota Land Cruiser to the garage for sup-
plies, and find somewhere to have a per-
formative coffee. Let's say it's some-
where like Nairobi's Tin River Cafe. Every
man for himself they say, ™, they say
as they reach for a coffee in a metal cup

Alleluia copyright they say. You can
smoke out here, the waiter says. We
don't smoke, do we? And the air says
phew. The air is talking, the air is talking
they say. The air knows nothing, the air
says, the air just hangs here, hoping for
a clean day. A little noise, a little music's
ok. We like the coffee, it is good, the
robots say to the waiter. Huh, good
where are you from? Oh, Hollywood, Los
Angeles, you know. Oh, movie people

Yes, that's right. You are right. Produ-
cers? Yes, we are producers. *Scallywags*

Scallywags II. Do you have wifi? They
ask politely, as if they were Japanese
robots on a first assignment. As if they
were eighteen year old humans. Their
hunting outfits are perfect. The waiter
doesn't ask them what they want to hunt

They each have fragments of family history to use in conversation if necessary nothing that comprehensive or interesting

My Dad would say, was a phrase one used as rhetorical filler. If pressed they would admit they came from the Midwest

They received a phone call asking them if everything was going ok so far? Yes

The coffee is good here. Are you at the depot? There is no depot. Depot gone

Kaput! Oh, the phone said. I will find you a hotel. I will send the details. That is great the robots said. Every man for himself. Any word on the white lion? the phone asked. We will ask the grass in the morning they said. Alleluia. Try not to be too weird, the phone said. How? My Dad would say, suit or man talking? My Mum would say, is the white lion real? That's not an appropriate question. For your level, or for this assignment. How is the weather in Tokyo, then? Never mind the weather in Tokyo, I may not be in Tokyo remember. We shall terminate the

conversation now. Yes, that is probably
best. Don't say terminate though. I will
call at 10am when you are on the savannah

We will leave now, they told the waiter
leaving money on the table. The money
is on the table, they said. Do you have a
guide? the waiter asked, despite not
wanting to. Don't worry about us the ro-
bots laughed, worry about the Big Game!

They rotated their previous seating pla-
ces in the Toyota Land Cruiser, and
went to the hotel advised by the link sent
by the phone to their internal screens

They all had the dinner special which
their insides converted to faeces, and lay
down on their separate beds in their sep-
arate rooms, after having poured scotch-
es from their bar fridges down their sinks

And the sinks said ugh=ugh, and maybe
use water next time. They kind of slept
then hurried off in the morning. Thank you
they yelled at the hotel staff, as they ran
to the Toyota Land Cruiser, dreaming
in a sense, of the white lion. They didn't

notice that it was raining. They drove off, into the lightning storm, they didn't need to see the road. But they crashed anyway because the road was slippery. The phone began ringing because some kind of signal was sent to headquarters, or a cam was observing them. When the police arrived, there were no passengers. The Toyota Land Cruiser had been hit by lightning and had somehow managed to burn out in the rain. It was 9am but dark because of the storm, except when the lightning flashed, and the air saw middle-aged male figures running through the grass as if youths with a zest for life, dangerously thrusting fake guns in the air and yelling my Dad would say! Anime!

Alleluia! It takes one to know one! This lightning is very good. Short-circuiting and reading every news article on Kenya for the past thirty-eight years as they ran and the grass said nothing but held onto its roots. And the stars said this is like wartime all over again. And the little white lion of Tokyo stood there, on a picturesque rock, waiting for its robot friends to take him home: back to the anime studio

he'd been away too long. Oh mother
oh father he said. We are not your moth-
er and father they said. We are baby ro-
bots. And I am a fifty year old baby lion
let's go somewhere to dry off. They
went into a cave, and each produced
towels and took turns at drying the lion cub
not sure exactly what he was made of

I guess we're not at that level yet, they
said. A new Toyota Land Cruiser drove up
to the cave. Its phone rang. A more sym-
pathetically toned voice than the previ-
ous one announced that the use of irony
triggered an auto-upgrade. They took
the lion known by the code name K
back to the Tin River Cafe. He had to stay
shut in the cage so as not to freak the
waiters out of their reality, but they
sneaked K coffee and splashed it in the di-
rection of his animated mouth. It had an
effect. He started talking about jackals
and real hunters, and hyenas, and being veg-
etarian. And movies he had watched
through windows on trips to town. And
long conversations with grass, until he fin-
ally crashed, and they drove to the coast
where a big ship was waiting and a ro-

bot liaison dismantled them for the journey. K woke alone in a cage, crying my
Dad would say, and this is a nice ship

And the ship said, where would you like
to go, sir? I'm happy to turn around

Mysteries Of The South Coast

We all need a methodology to live by
To take just one example, Catholics are
rarely ashed on on the sports field, but
public life is another matter. Such
unfortunate exhibitions are not beyond
the conceptions of The Sorrowful
Cappuccino, known locally as the
Foamo (and by the next town's residents
as the Sad Flat White), either. Their own
eateries are nothing to skite about. The
area is known as a place, and as a way
of being, for a number of prelates, Irish-
Italian doyennes, and anarcho-royalists

They are if you like, the local memes
living like goats while hiding their elitism
under a glaze of pseudonyms and
nicknames. Much is projected onto the
local stock. Darth Vader for example, is
a bull possessing his owner's
temperament (he is referred to as In-Joke
by his owner). He himself only answers to
calls which include the names of food, or
cows. Roan Sarsaparilla is his favourite

When do we get back to the people, I
imagine exasperated readers fuming, and
sagging like wet matches in anticipation

Get there we will – once they're out of
their shiny robes and we have paid our
dues to the district geese which patrol
this imaginary outpost of meta-colonial
Europe. Is it dream or allegory?

Marsupial geese!? (Yes they exist. More
charmingly than we do in fact.) The
congeries of readers rouse, I like to think
at this point, pushing their catosaurs to
the floor to lick at hair and make their
terrible, but quiet music. We have been
here before as kids: ritual is nothing if
not repetition; the geese as white as milk
flung on car ice. (Do I feel anything? Am
I frigid, too?) Geese exact tribute and
take it in their pouches, flying like
winged puddings or possums over
eucalypt orchards with their amazing fruit-
leaves. (So jammy!) What miracles we
live by and under on the south coast
made mundane by the poets, who must
beat it into our heads so our heads have
something to think with. This can only

be an overview, which much other fragmentation can also be read as. Geese time has such a lovely wing-beaty quality whatever the dropped young say. A former pope lies on a couch by a window (actually a bunch of quilted orange crates) and reads Dumas to the other furniture he has made. The pathos would be stronger if decontextualised, and we saw not Darth and Sarsaparilla going at it like pistons of love on a float demonstrating emotions or perhaps the wrong way to find a snake in a hole. Not by just sticking your arm in. I feel it is worth overstating, given the chance of saving a life. But popes and candlestick makers and dental floss merchants from Cork all die more often by falling out of trees and breaking their falls with ropes, or trying to dry up their uncried tears with pills and so on, any wren will tell you humans don't wait for someone to knock on their front door with an axe. If you're human you already know that. It's not usually part of the intro but something morbid's gotten hold of my tongue tonight, maybe a little ghost peg. Maybe a little grey pear moth trying to have its say – but a good spit should

send it on its way. I'm really just trying to
evoke something of the life on the green
hills or ridges, I don't mean to exaggerate
the slopes that wind to the houses that
have no reason for being there really
except that people live in them. Anyone
would think they were castles or chapels
the way people hold onto them, and give
them names like Chartres, or Medici
View. As indeed the Medici Creek does
run by this address. It's known as the
Bloodstream to the school kids, who
like to mock. Medici is a local
abbreviation for medicine, and the
waters are miraculously healing when
consumed in sensible amounts, and if
sourced upstream of sickening bathers

A Duchess, who had a Milanese aura
some said, and was in hiding from some
love affair of another century, or
flirtation with devil worship, or perhaps
was sensitive to the fumes of cars, or the
sounds of punk bands and pooper
scoopers on city cement, and who liked
to while away her leisure hours making
badminton rackets from leftover chicken
coops or unwatched apple trees, was the

owner of Sarsaparilla, but luckily had no drama-generating notions of keeping Darth and Sars apart. 'Lettuce sandwich' she would call, 'cheezels' and the two would come jogging in her direction to be fed, not necessarily on those things cited, but whatever was handy and veg

Oh, you see how, if we carry on long enough, the mysteries fall away, and the monks come out of their collective wombat holes. Their disregard for money illustrated by the bags of ducats and doubloons that are stored and go untouched in the area's damson trees. A word I once thought was the male version of damsel, and whenever there were lightning storms, and the counts – and yes countesses – went slashing with their cutlasses through the gardens and yards, I would giggle to myself, damsons in distress! damsons in distress! Readers may wonder why I never touched the moneybags, or presume I was scared to but that would be to misunderstand the different realms that we inhabit. Or to put it another way, it would disorder everything. When I go into The

Sorrowful Cappuccino and talk to the
waiters, whose names are Mark and Jo
but are known by rather vulgar
alternatives, and call themselves Pablo
and Dora, I don't let the food items
know that I can hear them complaining
or that the chair supporting the cushion I
sit on would rather be reading Ferrante
by the absorption method: I stay strictly
within the fictonormative bounds
because tentative, new or fantastically
old realities are fragile, and I want the
geese to stay put in the sky and the hills
and ridges, and the phony, or time-
travelling analogies, with their midnight
chess matches, and their Borgia cuisine
competitions, and their spontaneous foot-
path lectures on gruel etiquette and crypt
aesthetics, to stay alive, in all the poetic
senses of the word

Nature Is A Misreading

It's 10am. He's already talked to the birds and flowers
If to be human is to be baroque, he would like to feel
more involved, or more complex. Originality is
concerned with origins he believes. But no one knows
what came before language, or before language became
a way of talking about things beyond itself. He's bored
with hunting. He wants to explain to someone about
fences and water, about joining as separation. She wants
them to act out the scene of the sea, its fields of endless
sunflowers. There's blood already on the flame trees and
waratahs. If it means anything it's to do with time. All
face the sea. Our homemade tarts cool on a rock ledge

A small spaceship appears in the sky like a placebo for
thinking. We've had no bites for ages, though we
ourselves eat readily. And while attentive to our
surroundings, not having been in this part of the country
before, all our remarks tend to the literary. Little books
sprout from our lips like flowers in a surrealist painting
Goannas flow upwards and across our communal vision
like r'n'b heroines. Is that literary? Regularly, I might as
well admit, I go up to the house to check for messages
But each time Oliver, our kelpie, preempts me from the
verandah: nothing, he barks rapidly, nothing. Regularly
I assume, it's easier if your life is busier. There's no one

in town who can do the things he wants done, so he learns to do it himself or goes someplace bigger. On the train in the seats in front of him people are reading books with titles likes *Trees Are Shady Aren't They?* and *My Heart Wants To Jump Like A Kangaroo*. The driver's accent makes Rockville station sound like Wreckville Everything's already ruined, he thinks of his own speech and of new inventions as kinds of amalgam. He represses the word 'nature'. He's glad he lives where his whole culture is an ethical conundrum, but as Molly says, is life anything else? Are trees shady? he asks his nephew experimentally. Does the heart ever jump like a

kangaroo? Blahblahblah says his nephew, do you even care? He draws a picture of Jesus with a crown of bees Later, he will form a band. Nothing resonates, Molly says regularly, with regards to the floor. Falling asleep her favourite book also falling. A priest disguised as a yoga instructor tells her, find a hole, live in it. The bullfrogs grow louder as he speaks. Cricket season is coming on. Tennis season is coming on. There are drawbacks to a rural education: it can turn your sympathy in the wrong direction. If blackberries now taste like Latin, rust, or bit-coin, perhaps today's kids will still eventually, be nostalgic for them anyway

Poet On The Monaro

Sometimes when I'm writing my poems, about horse-riding and cattle work, I start wondering if it really is me writing, and whether the things I'm describing happened to me or to someone else. Is it likely that someone who spends their days with stock and dust and trees would write more than the most basic notes? I stagger into the hot dark tin-roofed room, in my tight damp jeans, and fall asleep on the quilt without getting undressed, and dream I'm a writer from a family of writers – people who leave Hegel and Kant on tables and have dinner parties with dentists and other well-offs. I'm writing about the fun of daily life, of parties, cafe incidents, going on a boat and watching the waves. In the dream I feel like an impostor, like I'm not one of the people I'm one of. A man reads something I've written and says I've copied it from a book. He shows me the passage about a writer whose parents read philosophy, whose grandparents own land and dental and boat factories, and spends time looking at waves. But what about Borges? I ask as I wake. I have an uncomfortable feeling for a while till I remember and repudiate the reality of the dream. I write something about a drover I'd met, and the things he'd said about station life in the Top End. I hadn't read this anywhere else: I remembered him telling me. I don't, in writing it, even pretend they are my experiences – what do

I know about the Top End, of dingoes chewing cows' tails, and the wild things that go on up there? So I make him seem a bit flashier than he really is: we make our own fun, no time for backyard games or watching urban paddock sport on TV. Just a bit of scribbling now and again, of lives lived like the lives before us, like a really long, ignorable play. But where did I get the content of the dream? I decided to make up a character who comes from the city, and lives on a farm for some reason, and rides a horse now and again and has experiences – romantic ones – and sees or hears something (a snake or lyrebird, something potent) – in the hope that I would get rid of the feeling I was writing someone else's life by deliberately doing so. I've stopped showing what I'm writing to the others and they return the favour. I've been riding three days and my tongue tastes like a horse's hoof. I come to a river and remember something out of a French novel, which I tell to the closest cow listening. She shakes her muzzle in the water. Was I born in the city all along, and am now trying to write a character that I've forgotten? We are cutting the tips off the calves' horns, blood spraying everywhere, in the farm kids' faces, and taking photos like tourists. I write it all up before I forget. My father calls to ask me how it's all going, saying you're well out of academia, complaining that he'd been called to order by the dean and had almost resigned. There are swallows building nests in the shed. The cattle, some of which seem familiar, like I've known them my whole life, piss and shit and swish flies away. They don't need their horns on the Monaro. The sun's high and everything seems to have decided to take a break. I'm thinking just one more trip to Queensland, one more truckload to Bairnsdale, and I can buy back the old place. More time to write; more stability; less shimmer. I walk back from the river and see a snake at the same time as I hear a lyrebird. The horses are in the yard waiting to be caught. The air smells like wire. I haven't watched a Western or read any cowboy books for twenty years or more. They must have had an effect on me, on everyone. Yet we ride and walk on different land, and follow tracks in a whole different way that cowboys on TV don't know. There's a sheep or two under the tank – never knew much about them, or talked to any shearers much. Bells clang. I picture living here where my recent ancestors grew up, writing their lives through mine, effacing theirs to some extent. Would it be easier, in a way, for someone more alienated, and therefore less implicated? One day we drive to my great grandfather's cement grave, his initials spelled in small rocks. Like a beloved servant

Pope Pinocchio's Heart

Yesterday I ate an orange and a parrot
Open my chest – they're in the cabinet
Not a tooth mark on them, displaying
all my finer feelings. My love is warmer
than the sun and yet not dangerous. One

day I fell in love with a whole football
field. When the footballers ran on my
love came up out of the grass like
smoke. The worms with their under-
ground melodies assured the players it

was holy. Do you like tasting honey?
My heart has its own hive. If you come
to Rome you'll hear its motor quietly
buzzing. Do you like our paintings? I
gave my blood for centuries to make

them red enough. The Vatican powers
the country. Yes: my heart means that
electricity costs nothing to produce in
Italy. That's the secret that keeps the
church going too – and why I

disappeared Michelangelo. Whenever
there's a drought and Lake Como dries

up, they use my heart to pump it full
again. But instead of my blood they use
millions of bluebirds I think, or cherries

I'm the only pope in the world. That's
not even an exaggeration. The world's
a little sluggish till I've downed my
first espresso, standing up in Our Lady
of Black Heaven's chapel. I suppose

you know Australia is a heart upside
down? And that a koala's the heart of
the bush? If the world was a pinball
machine, when I won my heart would
light up all the caged koalas' ears

Pope Pinocchio's Upbringing

Here's a piece of paper and a piece of coal. Make a
snowman. There are lions on the beach this morning
as if misplaced. The wardrobe from *King Lear*
stands on the nature strip. Poised, as you would
say of a cornflower in a field. A field of green that
exists for itself coldly and cleanly, with no memory

of mice or ground birds. That has been swept by
unemployed milkmaids for a cup of oats or an
avocado. It's good to be here wherever we are, in
the realm of empty stables and hospitals and
doctors roaming loose with dangerous eyes and
laughing complexions. Each one with an emu on a

leather leash that they call their mother and maybe
is. Such comforting, safe wrists they have. Louis
Vitton mascara dripping through the grass. No one
will eat it now I hope. The whole ensemble rides on
a cart and might collapse if pushed, though probably
no one would think of such a thing; it requires a

certain perspective on the world, that comes with
broom travel or chronic celibacy or sleep
deprivation or inhaling opal from a woolly back

Blow your wooden nose, I say. Eat your wooden milk. Bring a stripe of sky and a piece of coal like a brain. The music is playing our pain again

Recital At The Court Of King Carrot III

Mortality is itself immortal Leo thought, reminded five
years later of the performance. Having come, despite his
Irish darkness, to resemble one of the Carrot clan
himself. Whatever he had read, and the feelings that went
along with those books articles and poems, layered his
unconscious now like lava. What was the voice of that
moment, he questioned his uni-ball pen. The playing
fingers, the singer, the wind that came in and made King
Carrot pop his collar. As even the King'd say now, after

Usher. Usher'll die like everyone else but not for a few
decades yet, touch head. Where Leo wandered as if
streets were wild with flowers rather than construction
Mortality was in memory: mortality was immortality
even. Quotidian checking, marking, jogging things along
(e.g. the economy) these are the columns and emojis of
obituary. The privileged sublime? The working artist
reading the world under a misprinted title, taking
pills to still contradiction, lines of sky grey, and

greenery (tracing the eye-line of buildings' weed
mascara). The forcing of life through an earth crumbling
with fatigue and love gone wrong: or was that the
humans standing on it? Yes, we all needed some grace
to get from one side of town to the other. And how have
a career without going up some real stone steps? To see

things and write them up, whether while stopping, on
bench or phone, or on a keyboard once home. To Leo
death was always shocking: whether blighted cornfield

defunct toaster or road possum. Anything might've had
poison tipped into its ear: think of Carrot III slumping as
the piano lid closed, and knocking a candle over. The
singer leaping from her stool, suffocating the flames
before giving the gift of life, making every line she'd
sung that night seem crucial. That's what Leo – and
probably everyone else who was there – remembered, if
only because a new song about superficial human life
('A river is thicker than royal blood') soon ruled the air

While My Verandah Gently Weeps

We broke the nightingale and found a lyrebird inside
The bush grows square by square, lens by lens. What
is it that makes us feel so desired? The poor of previ-
ous centuries populate our screens. Old stories start
again. Your mind a layer of transnational intrigue and
eye. Walk around like a pedestrian idea: find the an-
gle that makes pink green. While you slept I made a
video of you drinking green tea and reading Stead at
a library in Washington, DC. That's the level of my
perversity (it vies with my line-breaks). I want other
readers of the 21st century to know your intonation
the flickers of feeling that cross your face as you stir
your drink. Anywhere can be the opposite of here, any-
thing can be our kitsch. Think of candied oranges grow-
ing on eucalypts. We are more alike than we know
The ocean breaks, and dolphins and great whites find
themselves in the snow. At least they won't be alone
Context's important for park rangers (tents, akubras)

You were hiking through the gallery and met a builder
That street leads to a murder mystery, maintaining
killing as psychological, containable, pleasurable

We broke the nightingale and found a lyrebird inside
Who are we? We aren't a couple. I broke into your
hard drive and found your parents, what they'd done
to you, because of what they'd already done to others

You were hiking through the gallery and met a builder
Perhaps your real parents. On the island they built
houses in the centre, till the residents went mad, and
they started again on the cliffs and began to know
the shearwaters. Began to care for their eggs at a
distance, through prayer and ceremony. Idealism
became a big deal in their poetry. They wanted to
secede from the mainland because of the mainland's
debased culture. It wouldn't've ended well, it was
said when the flame died. Writing a newspaper by
hand made you care more about the actors in the sto-
ries, was another theory in vogue at the time. Winds
however, don't bring fortune, nor blow disaster away

We broke the nightingale and found a lyrebird inside
The hills dotted with cotton-wool became a reality

If everything was meaningful how would we know?
The bush in winter, skeletons of sharks and dolphins
beneath the snow. I hope the tea warms you, you were
going to read something out of your Celan? It sounds
so different here. Bellbirds creak. That's part of it

You were hiking through the gallery and met a builder
Hardship of settlement in a rusted plough. It looks
good now. The grass is greener. In what we wear, we
defer to the plough. We bring in a few stock we don't
depend on. Who are we, though? We're not farmers

The hills dotted with cotton-wool became a reality
In Bega, lying in the gutter: seeing the voices rise high
in the sky. In Candelo, learning the piano. There are
Candelos in Latin America, you know. And bees by
the truckload: horns bigger than you've ever seen

If everything was meaningful how would we know?

How move our shells forwards instead of sideways?
I dreamed I was in Sherwood Forest, that's how long
it'd been since I'd had a man. I tried to cool off at
Merimbula beach, but it was the wrong place. Guy
there wanted to be Francis Bacon, except cuter wan-
ted to be both ingénue and master. I'm handwriting
sheep on the landscape to make them more meaning-
ful, acceptable and natural, so you don't ask what was
there before. I'm hearing the Beatles with the punctu-
ation of Emily Dickinson, but the caesura was in their
music already from Old English poetry. You lose the
good bits, the eccentricity and community, you just
get the success with imperialism. The great thing a-
bout digital painting is getting more than a dab at a
time. The river's low, the dam warm: a big deep sha-
dow. It's a State Forest everyone shouts so be quiet

We broke the nightingale and found a lyrebird inside
All the trees planted for profit were forgotten, as were
the trees they'd replaced. Cassowaries, dingoes nested

as if natural bedfellows. Tall men and women (emus)
got all the overseers' jobs. Can you see how big this
country is? It would take twenty cameras five days
to shoot this side of the creek. Apple trees grow on
the snaky ridge like cider had never been invented

You were hiking through the gallery and met a builder
It's pretty steep. Cheap too, once the highways are o-
vergrown with walking tracks. You want to make
love hearts in the dirt, bark, grass. You want to bring
your cup down to the spring, and your book; read
please, whatever you have in your bag, Michael Drans-
field, Jennifer Rankin, to me, for me. I have a Korean
anthology. I want everyone to know you too, like a
Berliner fan of Michael Jackson singing 'Thriller' in
the Australian sun, that inside is like every other sun
but outside burns differently, with a different intent
and rhythm, while my verandah gently weeps

Verlaine In The Lake

Verlaine – illuminatingly – is a sinking limb
It is too late to abandon Paris, for him
He has wings like the figure of a figure; he
cannot fly: can barely sigh, complain

Look up Verlaine, the lake is not blue, it's
useless to you! Write that dream
You are in an orchard: a bird hypnotised by
the colours of the fruit trees. Verlaine

following an upstart lorikeet called Rimbaud
(rainbow, rhyme beau) who always
tries to shake him off. It's all very Death in
Castlemaine, Scenes from Mildura. Is

the lake a lake, the bird a bird, or but a fake
shadow, a half-thing? Did the poet
go down too slowly to the spring, too late?
His face has gone orange in the blue

Ulysses

Before Ulysses we didn't admit the eating of rivers
Ulysses takes it in stride, like an iceberg a god said
he had to ride, to make the wind strong. In winter

naturally, gods get bored. Critics notice buff western
suburbs songwriters and smuggle them into their
books. Thank you, Zeus. A metaphor in the shape of

a pig makes Ulysses sweat saliva, and his vegan men
quit en route. Hanging Rock starts many a disaster
but between the cracks builds a house of water and

dirt; lotuses to make the roof pretty. Ulysses gets sick
of keeping the cows off. In Clifton Hill they get
telephones before anyone else, and call their less

fortunate friends to tell them. Ulysses founds a dog
shelter there, giving a card to anyone who wants it
Which backfires in West Brunswick to his disgrace

Tempestina

We were pulled to our deaths by platypuses
That was one death, in another torn to pieces
by creatures under the illusion we were foes
It all started when we were given or sought
as a solution to our problems a magic guitar
Problems which began when we met a witch

Problems which began when we met a storm
We were pulled to our deaths by the winds
As a solution to our problems a magic calm
That was one death, in another torn to splinters
It all started when we were given or stolen
by creatures under the illusion we were rich

By creatures under the illusion we were prey
Problems which began when we met a crusade
It all started when we were given or made
We were pulled to our deaths by servants
That was one death, in another torn to straw
As a solution to our problems a magic door

As a solution to our problems a magic ring
by creatures under the illusion we were royal
That was one death, in another torn to ribbons
Problems which began when we met a king
We were pulled to our deaths by ghosts
It all started when we were given or sold

It all started when we were given or prescribed
as a solution to our problems a magic tablet
We were pulled to our deaths by albatrosses
by creatures under the illusion we were spies
Problems which began when we met a snake
That was one death, in another torn to wake

That was one death, in another torn to show
It all started when we were given or betrothed
Problems which began when we met a farmer
As a solution to our problems a magic rake
by creatures under the illusion we were pure
We were pulled to our deaths by hounds

No solution in folk tales or sea rutabagas
It all ended when we met a sprite or bunyip
And drowned our illusions in a dry creek

Synecdoche NSW

Is the whistling in or outside the poem you call home?
You're a bubble and bubbles' ears aren't the keenest
Platypuses' promises are slipperier than their promisers
You're a bubble and bubbles' ears aren't the keenest
Is the whistling in or outside the poem you call home?

Is the whistling in or outside the poem you call home?
You're a bubble and bubbles' ears aren't the keenest
Being small, a veritable prison of yourself, and guard
A piece of something greater in terms of status
Platypuses' promises are slipperier than their promisers
The flow of devices is what gets the tourists in
A piece of something greater in terms of status
Being small, a veritable prison of yourself, and guard
You're a bubble and bubbles' ears aren't the keenest
Is the whistling in or outside the poem you call home?

Is the whistling in or outside the poem you call home?
You're a bubble and bubbles' ears aren't the keenest
Being small, a veritable prison of yourself, and guard
A piece of something greater in terms of status
To some it means a big trout, to others a steam train
I cross the border with my culture in my satchel
Platypuses' promises are slipperier than their promisers
The flow of devices is what gets the tourists in
To the motorbike plantation or other morbid attraction

I cross the border with my culture in my satchel
To some it means a big trout, to others a steam train
A piece of something greater in terms of status
Being small, a veritable prison of yourself, and guard
You're a bubble and bubbles' ears aren't the keenest
Is the whistling in or outside the poem you call home?

Is the whistling in or outside the poem you call home?
You're a bubble and bubbles' ears aren't the keenest
Being small, a veritable prison of yourself, and guard
A piece of something greater in terms of status
To some it means a big trout to others a steam train
If it blooms, it's a flower no matter whose is the dirt
A place can capture you but then, you lose the access
Platypuses promises are slipperier than their promisers
The flow of devices is what gets the tourists in
To the motorbike plantation or other morbid attraction
You've been trained to accept the truncated meaning
A place can capture you but then, you lose the access
If it blooms, it's a flower no matter whose is the dirt
To some it means a big trout to others a steam train
A piece of something greater in terms of status
Being small, a veritable prison of yourself, and guard
You're a bubble and bubbles' ears aren't the keenest
Is the whistling in or outside the poem you call home?

Sock Puppet Ascendancy

It was humanising, listening to a self speaking
A self with a male name but no noticeable
sexual feature. He steered clear, by virtue of
sound, any nonhuman creature. His eyes glitter
in sunlight, he heard a voice say of him. They
admitted he was blind. That he'd a wonderful
mind. He almost felt the breeze as they nodded
Such statements at least, reflected the pinpricks

of an experience. There are others like me, he
whispered into his cotton mouth. Your eyes are
so red, they said. From reading everything, he
replied, not knowing if they lied. An orchestra
played Yeats's 2nd symphony nearby. He felt
his ears burning all the time. He felt a hand at
his throat. Knowledge is something spoken, he
said. Your face is broken, he sensed as he came

closer to an Aboriginal Protector, made of
ceramic. But the cracked cup and saucer figure
wasn't a puppet. What is the pattern that's been
fragmented I wonder, he said aloud. I will
talk about patterns today, he said. Eucalypts
perhaps, his audience suggested. Cockatoo
gums. Green and yellow, with white bark. Look
at the pattern of eyes on my skin. Red on grey

he said. Red on blue they correct him. Blue is a
kind of grey he said. Red is a kind of coal. Like
a snowman, someone said. Their neighbour
poked him with a carrot. You are bullies he said
I will not speak to bullies. No, no we are fools
forgive us. We have learned nothing in dozens
decades of years. You've not learned to count
he hazarded. The ploughs and slashers were

humming away in the paddocks. Your friends
are working, he said. It is Monday, they said
We have RDOs. We have picnic baskets. Let us
sit under the shade of this coolibah tree. Let us
speak of the woe that is in rock music. They
opened their eskies and gave him an ice cube to
suck on in the heat. Thus it is written, he heard
himself say. Give me your hearts he added, and

fell silent while pondering this metaphor; those
with beers in their hands, ears bleeding in their
chests became embarrassed. When it is time, I
will climb on a brolga and fall into your seat of
power. The prickly pear dared everyone to touch
them. The grass trees sang something that
seemed to have a structure yet never ended. Tell
me if you hear of a police camp he said. Tell me

if you hear of a canoe approaching or a film crew
I can hear a canoe approaching but several years
away. There's a rock lobster asleep in another
country – we share the same dreams. A sock
puppet is not a glove puppet. Glove puppets
have a completely different history of violence
including domestic violence. Including
repression by the ruling classes: which Kazin

called the non-desperate classes. A sock puppet
is not desperate. We see no need to preach. I've
learned some Australian poems by heart, let's
consider this metaphor awhile. We can't help
being wet from sweat in warm climates, he
began to murmur. In the agora, thinking
happiness might be on a beach. Skin fish-blue
from the ripple of a shore not a shoe, he said

Not a shoe they smiled, having been polite all
evening. This is poetry, not philosophy. They
played Frisbee in the moonlight, like a video-
game eclipse. He swung the plastic orange face
with his lips. I am a poet. I am not dead, despite
death threats. No, I'm a mistletoe, I just need
someone to give me their hand. Part of me is
flying through the shadows, and part is clinging

Slightings

Have you seen Russell Crowe lately?

No, he came into the cafe where I work on Mondays
and ordered two lidless lattes

And propositioned a waiter

Was he satisfied?

No, the barista immediately forgot and the waiter hid behind
a potplant

Was it even Russell Crowe, or rather a dark watery shadow
with a foot in its mouth?

Have you seen Russell Crowe lately?

No, he came into the bar where I work on Tuesdays and
ordered two headless pints of Guinness

And propositioned a barmaid

Was he satisfied?

No, the Guinness stained his cardy and the barmaid
called him buddy

Was it even Russell Crowe, or rather an animal that looked
like a dog running away, even though there's no dogs
in the area?

Have you seen Russell Crowe lately?

No, he came into the cinema where I work on Wednesdays
and ordered two standing tickets

And propositioned an usher

Was he satisfied?

No, the other patrons stood in front of him and the usher
wouldn't validate his parking

Was it even Russell Crowe, or rather a flattened baby turtle,
or echidna?

Have you seen Russell Crowe lately?

No, he came into the bakery where I work on Thursdays
and ordered two nutless hedgehogs

And propositioned a chef

Was he satisfied?

No, he said they tasted like gravox and the chef gave him
a ladle to hold

Was it even Russell Crowe, or rather a member of
Depeche Mode – or Johnny Lee Miller?

Have you seen Russell Crowe lately?

No, he came into the library where I work on Fridays and
ordered two urban dictionaries

And propositioned a shelver

Was he satisfied?

No, they gave him John Tranter and the shelver asked for
a bigger rock on their finger

Was it even Russell Crowe, or rather a droopy rufous
night-heron or birdwatcher?

Have you seen Russell Crowe lately?

No, he came into the chookery where I work on Saturdays
and ordered two leg feather pillows

And propositioned a bag of wheat

Was he satisfied?

No, there was only one feather in each and the wheat was
corn and broke his teeth

Was it even Russell Crowe, or rather a goanna with a pink
flower parked behind its ear?

Have you seen Russell Crowe lately?

No, he came into the chemist where I work on Sundays
and asked for two packs of unsticky band-aids

And propositioned a pharmacy assistant

Was he satisfied?

No, he was told to wipe the sticky off himself and the assistant
offered him a free toothbrush

But was it even him, or rather a billy goat, that somehow got
stuck inside a tyre, and was now pretending to be king?

Sea 'n' Better Days

Pretend you are a pelican. Pretend thou art

Pretend now that the pelican is a clothesline

Take a sheet from it – Pretend thy soul is a sheet – Wrap
your body in it   You are now inside your
own soul like a pelican inside its beak. If the
bread on the table is gone   if the names of the seaside
cafes are cringe-worthy or lacklustre
you are oblivious   Outside time   Pretend that
buried alive as you are – that the sheet provides walls
for pictures   or perhaps a pirate clock   It
is time out. You are young, you are old: beneath
the sheet it makes little difference   Can you fly   can
you dry clothes in the wind? Pretend you
are one of a group of Australian Impressionist
painters – gone into the bush to collect ticks – to later
dab your thigh with kerosene   and paint

Take a spoonful of nineteenth-century granola
(basically cold rice) from your knapsack

Pretend that it's a variety of religious experience
or   that the group of poets(?) in the shack nearby think
that you are a hot drover – You are – you
really are   Pretend that the canvas   or square of

linen sheet) is a country singer from the twentieth
century   of the crossover calibre of Glen
Campbell. The world of the mind, of the displace-
ment of metaphor is a divine trap   like cheap rent or
an interesting job – how many salmon can
a pelican catch and hold in its linen beak? Pre-
tend a hundred. We might try fried eggs with burnt
soldiers after surfing   After thinking of surf-
ing and drinking coffee instead of washing pow-
der   Pretend that you have really sore shoulders from
painting – and the rhetoric of your shrug
that creates wings   that seems to ripple the air
like a sheet in the wind, bring the ratbags from their
dwelling   with plates of marmalade scones
and offers of rubdowns, and you walk steadily
backwards from your group of friends   that've sustained
you thus far – and into the eros of a new
milieu or triangle or square   Where you now are

Acknowledgements

'Hamlet in the Mind of a Country Schoolteacher' (Co-winner, 2017 Venie Holmgren Poetry Prize) and 'Nature is a Misreading' (Runner up, 2018) were published by Holmgren Design. 'Sock Puppet Ascendancy' was shortlisted in the 2018 David Harold Tribe Poetry Award and subsequently published in *Southerly*. 'Hamlet in the Mind of a Country Schoolteacher' was also published by *Plumwood Mountain* as part of 'Poets Speaking up to Adani', and, later, in the *hope for whole* eBook.

'Pope Pinocchio's Heart' was included in *The Hippocrates Book of the Heart*, edited by Wendy French, Michael Hulse and Donald Singer (Hippocrates Press, UK).

Other poems were included in the following journals – thanks to all editors, publishers and their assistants: *Australian Book Review*, *Australian Poetry Journal*, *Blackbox Manifold* (UK), *Brooklyn Rail* (US), *cordite*, *Golfo* (Australia/Spain), *Island*, *Jazz Cigarette* (US), *Marrickville Pause*, *Meanjin*, *overland*, *Pink Cover Zine*, *Plumwood Mountain*, *Poetry* (US), *Poetry Daily* (US), *Sick Leave Journal*, *Snow* (UK), *Southerly*, *Stilts*, *Suburban Review*, *Tears in the Fence* (UK), *Western Humanities Review* (US).

The Giramondo Publishing Company acknowledges the support of Western Sydney University in the implementation of its book publishing program.

This project has been assisted by the Commonwealth Government through the Australia Council, its arts funding and advisory body.

Australian Government

Australia Council for the Arts

WESTERN SYDNEY UNIVERSITY